Jungle Gyms for Monkey Minds
Poetry by Neil Kaufman

Praise for *Jungle Gyms for Monkey Minds*

"I like your poetic sensibilities, enjoy watching you work out logical ideas with a poetic heart."

— Christine Stephens-Krieger, Grand Rapids Poet Laureate, 2024-2027, author of *Love Garden at the End of the World*

"These poems aren't boring. Moving from earth and into space and back again, many of these offer insights into real life, not artifice. 'Knowing what matters is which side I'm on,' for instance. The result is a lyric intimacy."

— Robert VanderMolen, author of *Skin* and *Water*

"The title alone of Neil Kaufman's dizzying collection of poems, *Jungle Gyms for Monkey Minds*, alerts us that we are about to encounter a revelation of the unexpected. Early on we are moved from what we expect— 'You / can't see a conductor / of an orchestra / if you're only listening to the music / the orchestra / is playing' to 'Is it / so odd to suggest that some people / haven't been told about the existence / of conductors?' Kaufman creates a deconstructed world releasing reason and replacing it with 'surprise' be it playful, serious, or ominous. In intelligently syncopated lines, phrases and structures, Kaufman creates both the impact of impermanence and also the daily challenges of facing the unexpected. Near the end, Kaufman writes that he himself spends much time recuperating from mental overwork doing what most 'are largely unaware of . . .' Neil Kaufman dares us to be aware."

— Jack Ridl, author of *All At Once*, and *Practicing to Walk Like a Heron*

"Neil Kaufman's work in his first book initially may strike one as 'quirky,' but I suggest that he is charting a new version of traditional fables such as those by Marie de France and Jean de La Fontaine, perhaps too the bestiary, most recently seen in Pablo Neruda's *Bestiario*. Such works require that the reader possess both a childlike 'monkey mind' and the adult sophistication that can grasp the messages of the work. When you come to Neil's first book, be prepared for delight in both. Beyond that, his work shows a tendency to play with binary opposites, and explores connections to spirituality and the problems with those whose rigidity prevents seeking the spirit from acceptance of others. His book is far more complex than a first reading may show."

— David Cope, Grand Rapids Poet Laureate 2011-2014,
author of *Moonlight Rose in Blue*

"I don't read poetry but I read Neil Kaufman."

— Andrew Noe, bank teller and gamer

ISBN 978-1-968226-04-6

Grand River Poetry Press
Grand Rapids, Michigan, USA
grandriverpoetrycollective.com

dedicated to Thalia and Myles

Table of Contents

Foreword

Hang, pull, grip, swing, fall, land like a cat.

Neil Kaufman begins with a soft open. Instructions to the artist regarding the manner in which one may navigate the nerve net of the creative process. This Jungle Gym. Familiar, yet daunting. Full of joy commingled with potential self immolation.

Is each creative act pre-cognition? Are we doing God's work by watching the world? Does a symbiotic relationship exist between matrix and maker?

After my first read through of Kaufman's collection, I was struck by the feeling that Neil had led me deep into a forest leaving markers on tree trunks and boulders so as to facilitate our finding our way back to a familiar clearing. Each marker, a poem. However, somewhere along the way the path shifts. Kaufman's poems lead us back to the forest's perimeter, then takes a sharp turn towards a clearing familiar to him, perhaps not us. In this clearing resides his obstacle, his destination on a journey towards personal clarity and balance.

Along the way he takes us down clever rabbit trails.

A midnight jungle gym surrounded by candles.

Several Polaroids of childhood trauma.

The detritus of loneliness.

His trajectory of walking away from self destruction both metaphysical and physical.

You may find yourself as travel companion fighting the darkness preoccupied with the fragility of veins.

Expect to receive the calm grasp of his hand as you navigate this journey.

Anticipate understanding our shared struggles with technology as we spar with authenticity.

Feel free to laugh and smile broadly as he peppers his quest with humor and whimsy amidst scattered dystopian images.

Prepare for a new appreciation for perhaps yourself or others for whom you care that have struggled with obstacles impacting the mind and perception of a here and now already difficult to understand.

I found myself returning again to the collection to reexamine certain poems.

"crux," a delightful aside regarding the manner in which one may or may not disturb the universe. Previously published in "Voices."

"In Life, It's Important To:," unfolds a fun frolic in word play and conclusive possibilities. My favorite line perhaps being, "aspire to be a cartographer of rabbit trails."

"The Beggar in My Brain," a study in the tinsel strength of one's psyche attempting to attune to that inner world which more often than not appears indifferent to our obstacles.

In 2004, Neil Kaufman walked into a weekly poetry event I hosted at Morningstar 75, a hipster coffee house, once "ground zero" in Grand Rapids, Michigan. Like an angel that had wandered in from another galaxy, his love and support for other poets palpable and sincere. Throughout the years we have crossed paths, compared notes and worked on projects together. Neil has remained a constant. Affable in his disposition. Curious for growth. An innate practitioner of the principles of Kaizen. Much should have stopped him. But as many poets can testify, the will to create often forges the machination to continue. As such, he remains indomitable.

Greg Bliss

The Petal Painting Insect

There's a little bug
that lives in the stem
of every flower
who paints
the things it thinks,
feels and sees
on
the petals
before
they bloom,
so
if you ever need
to know
what's
on the world's mind,
just plant a flower,
give it plenty
of sustenance
and
you will see.

"Hope Is the Thing with Feathers"
(poem/prayer/prophecy)

replicate and sell
your wounded wings
charge a dime per feather
each feather
a poetic punch line
or prayer
penned on a leaf
of a dime-store notebook
you scrawl into
intermittently
day and night
in that vein
you find varicose inspiration
write a whole wing
if you're serious
about alchemizing
poems and prayers
into prophecies
write both wings
it'll cost more
but we'll get the big idea
pack a guitar
to sing prophetically
you've delivered
if your singing
has a special kind of ring
like perfect pitch
only more daring
stray blue notes
prophets agree
most prophecies
aren't put in motion
by their hands
whether whispered
affirmations

in private
or shouted clarion calls
in public
prophesied derive energy
listening and following through
prophet revered
earning stripes
mystery guests involved
bound together
in no particular order
like trapezists on trapezes
with no net beneath
how Heaven
entering the world
watched over
by God's goslings
works
because some
profess
God exists
as more
than a name
a word
an expletive

Flame Tickle Tackle

Please

let my flame tickle
your flame
in the inky dark,
in our inky dark,
in our ink

Let the dark shroud
envelope us

let it sink in

slowly feeding our
dancing blue flame

crux

walking along the steps
I met a toad, a bat and a butterfly
the toad croaked, the bat squeaked,
but the butterfly
made no sounds
of any kind
I figured
they were inquiring
why
I was on the steps
in the first place
to which I replied
to the toad,
"To jump,"
the bat,
"To fly,"
but I had
no answer
for the butterfly

so I sat
on a step
and thought
for a very
long
time

when I realized
the butterfly
had not asked
a question
at all

so
I did not give it an answer

and continued, embarrassed, up the stairs…

Velvet

I hugged you
in your black velvet
dress with the
many folds and stays
and as you enveloped me
with them

I could've sworn
I had fallen into a black
hole of velvet folds and stays,
wrinkles upon wrinkles of
soft, quiet velvet…

MISTAKE

The tears will melt the rust away that accumulated when I got lost without an umbrella or a poncho or a good waterproof seal even in the emerald and misty forest. The forest was in the backyard of my third childhood home and I kept finding toy soldiers or comic books and miniature race cars which inspired fog shapes and the sun just wouldn't go down and the borders of the woods just kept expanding until finally I found an old glow-in-the-dark band aid and then the sun had a reason to set. It was then I cried, small, alone with a bunch of toys but no playmates. When poison ivy got boring, you flew over and licked my cheek with your little bird's tongue and I swear I've never seen a bird I could hold in the palm of my hand shed so many tears, enough to fill up my pail with the discarded shovel and take a bath with. It was your song that convinced me to stop shoveling into the dead leaves, you know, dirt, worms and twigs of the forest floor when the itch and loneliness were so great I thought I would bury myself and live in the trees by feeding the nutrients that could still benefit someone into the ground.

white light

in a birdhouse of his own liking
vampire bats sucked the blood out of the canaries
dressed up in yellow feathers
but made the mistake of only flying around at night
all we had to do
was seize the moon
and out of nowhere came the sun
and, agitated, the bats flew back to their caves
and there we searched
with blinding white lights
which they flew to
like moths to a bare light bulb

mourning

I like the car better
with the lights off
trees are like veins
spreading through the air
oil is like tears
spilling out of our cars
I need to write it all down
but can't 'til the light's red
and by then the pedestrian signs
will be flashing
telephones spread across the sky
coffee's spilling onto my knees
I feel like I'm going to puke
but can't 'til the window's down
and even then
won't make it in time
to get the best parking spot
at the bicycle shop

cross-pollination

everything is a kind of flower,

and I'm a bee.

lately,

I've been turning

flowers into bees

and I'm a flower.

and I'm a bee.

and I'm a flower.

and I'm a bee.

and I'm a flower.

perfection to the 3rd degree, Y, and x-bound

heaven only thought it was hell for a minute
darkness descended
and turned it that way

before it knew better,
hell became infatuated with heaven
and both plunged into the lake,
side by side
making love-babies called human beings

human beings rained from the sky
into this tiny air pocket called Earth
and began procreating in a parallel fashion

before long,
little babies were popping out of the ground everywhere
and poppies and daylilies were very quick to follow

it wasn't until they all fused with one another
that the problems started,

and war,
    and hate,
        and anger,
            and fear,
                and sadness,
                    and unhappiness,
                        and confusion,
                            and hope

jay

while storms pass overhead
where do birds hide?

rarely do I see a dead robin
lying in the road

or blue eggs smashed
on the ground

and I have yet to encounter
a bird's nest
smashing up against
my windshield

perhaps I've been searching
down the wrong avenues

but then again,
maybe the road commission's doing a better job
than I think

hiding out
in passing tornadoes

sweeping all that is dead into the sky

Darkness Is as Light to You

It rained for eons. It rained so long,
people forgot how to make fire altogether.
It was so wet, people forgot what warmth was.
What dry could be. The atmospheric
conditions necessary for a slow burn.
Thoughts of light slowly waned from the world.
All lightning was extinguished.
People heard stories of fire,
but there are some things even
the best stories can't accurately convey
and if you've never seen it before,
fire is definitely one of them.
The moon went on pulling the tides,
but people forgot it, too,
so forever did clouds hang in the air.
The sun was not understood,
only grayness. Never since
has water been so taken for granted.

Laundering Purgatorial Purges

I found a spring. Every so often
A demon bird will pass by, causing me
To spew. By the end of it, I've sorted
Through the perjury looking for the spring
Only to find it into doing wash.

We Don't Know Each Other So Well That Technology Finishes Each Others' Sentences

how many would say they're psychic from watching TV shows
written by the delusional paid to wax psychotic
reinforced by masses carrying phones everywhere
    "plugged in"
    talking on them without discretion
something that once never left the house
and to most seemed a bit freakish when it did
compounded by
text messaging computer programs
automatically finishing words
typed in phones to one another

"How did it know how to finish that word?"
hearkens back to Maverick predicting the ace of spades
as well as stirring odd feelings when watching movies
about robots instead of people
whole flocks
flood to movie theaters to watch phone jokes en masse
if somebody's goes off everyone laughs and nobody minds

when not engaged in cellular conversation
who flinches at syllables
relative to what was said or typed into their phones
like a tic, like listeners' Tourette's
around designed conversations
thanks to surveyed demographics

from lack of stimulation
word limits cutting them short
tiny buttons to use
and the brain trying to reconcile egregious misspelling

until the phone is out again
searching through a barrage of advertisements
appearing instantly about what is typed

to provide more to complain over
charging more to their accounts

it's only a matter of time
'til they blurt out
some cell phone jargon
especially in public
trying to cover up slips of the tongue
by singing a song
or reading aloud, even singing, a nearby product description
which of course the corporations
also tailor to fit

some see if slipped syllables
of legalese they learned
from the crime-fighting psychic show
hit a nerve
of anyone around them
turned silent observers

handwritten grocery lists
on the rare occasion that that happens
come with declining spelling and penmanship
bringing about great tumults
over the wrong groceries
and the lost ability to write by hand

watch ricocheting tics
dazzle the floor at comic conventions
lit up like pinball machines
texting Dungeons and Dragons with one hand
sorting through rows of comics with the other
wait for the ridicule when he suggests
they use personal digital assistants
to get all of the comics in mint appearance electronically
in the parking lot

multitudes of customized license plates
crying talent over anything finished aptly,
crying super,
crying psychic,
crying God

Lightning's Path

When lightning's path
is chosen,
every step
seems calculated,
so particular is its course,
and even though it's anything
but straight,
it's beautiful
because it's full of light.

If a Tree Falls

if one lives like a tree
growing to the sun
and falls
only then do certain tree branches
finally get their fingers in the soil
with limbs
that had only ever reached skyward

Laugh Graft

we'd be invincible but that'd deprive doctors from healing
we'd read minds but that'd deprive poets from saying
and writing all that's on our minds
including what we'd be thinking for awhile into the future
so we'd have peace to not think b/c cheat sheets called poems
are 4 sale in their books
we'd pay poets more money than their very meager wages
but every time we did that before, they squandered it on xxx
and we share everything that we are by giving it back in death
all the blind would see but then some
would never teach us how to add new depths to our other senses
we'd only talk to communicate
but then we wouldn't have bargain corner ads
and comic strips in newspapers
and comic strip characters would rip pencils right out of their artists' hands
for some of the things they draw
but then we'd be crazy
but, crazy can be culture shock
and I have great difficulty finding that it's anything but
we'd all do whatever we'd want all the time
but never know the conjunction junction's function
and we'd all speak one language with no dialects
and only communicate one clear meaning at a time
but then no one would get new ideas from what we say incl. new jokes
and we'd be coordinated without flaw
but then no one would cry over spilled milk
so we'd never be able to say,
"There's no use crying over spilled milk."

being

$1 = -1 \times -1$

but

more importantly

$-1 \times -1 = 1$

and denying denial

is the only solution

which gives breadth of existence

in the tiny diamond mind

of a sparkling

intuitively designed

fully developed

and indefatigably withstanding

beautiful

human

being

identity

Don't Plant Giving Trees

Giving Trees attract
human beings who take like
parasitic weeds.

The Sound of Conductors

You
can't see a conductor
of an orchestra
if you're only listening to the music
the orchestra
is playing.

Is it
so odd to suggest that some people
haven't been told about the existence
of conductors?

No,
it's not.

Their perspectives
on the music
are worth hearing.

But
conductors exist
and the orchestra
needs one.

Poems That Don't Rust

Some poems don't rust because they're organic. They grow. They aren't manufactured. Some poems hurt when they grow, like with growing pains. Growing pains are attributed to growing up into the mature, adult body. There's a sheltered existence that some people become adults in, but some shelters rust. I prefer the forest, the storm. There's a phenomenon described as atmospheric ghost light, will-o'-the-wisp – ignis fatuus, or, translated from the Latin, "foolish fire" – present in bogs, marshes and swamps, attributed, in actuality, to the combustion of gas from decomposed matter. The Latin term also connotes a deceptive goal or hope. Superstition. Superstitions don't last; new ones are formed, old ones are banished to obscurity. There's another phenomenon of the dead, and of bogs, bog bodies, specific to peat bogs whereby some organic matter decomposes remarkably slowly. The skin, hair, nails and internal organs of a human body can be found there nearly intact decades after a person has died there. This is due to cold, acidic, oxygen-poor conditions. If I die in a peat bog, I hope you find this poem in the contents of my barely decomposed stomach like a message in a bottle, the words arranged as delicately as a ship in a bottle. I live on words. I consume them more than bread. The paper they're written on is full of fiber, they make up the fiber of my being. The words of my poems won't ignite and disappear forever, won't break down or rust.

vertical

I'm running
through a hall
bathed down
the middle
with a
brilliant white light
as I run past
every door
to the left
and the right
slams
when I reach
the tip
from which
the great light
shines
every door
will reopen
once more

and knowing
all that matters
is which side
I'm on

lighthouse

broken colors,
I refuse to alter my eyes for you
anymore
the diamonds in my mind
broke you up
until I forgot that they exist
and you,
the sun

slope

what started as
close your eyes and forge ahead
turned into
open your eyes and forge ahead
and the change happened
so gradually
it was almost
mathematical

In Life, It's Important To:

watch cartoons under a microscope,
detain no one on grounds of superstition,
study like an ophthalmologist
who specializes in identifying everything
that makes eyes play tricks,
develop a sixth sense for detecting what goes bump in the night,
own a precise seismograph
to measure everything anyone calls "groundbreaking,"
aspire to be a cartographer of rabbit trails,
enlightened in every aspect of what
makes people go on tangents,
keep your balance,
read fine print like large print and large print like fine print,
become a walking encyclopedia
concerning everything that makes the sky fall,
acquire second sight in case you lose your original sight,
write all things science fiction,
all science fiction seems to manifest itself into reality, eventually,
thereby making science fiction authors
the masters of saying, "I told you so,"
close any and all eyes in the back of your head,
accurately guess what's in the crystal ball
of any fortune teller sitting across from you,
expertly seek good produce at grocery stores,
and discover that you don't have to be superhuman to be humane.

zero

a million little hands springing forth from eyes
and their only aim is to grab onto mine
sunglasses have only left me in the dark
and what's the point of seeing
if you can't see the eyes of others
my best method has been to stare down the hands
or forgo the fact that they exist at all
and anyways, whenever they get too close
they always end up burning their digits

Bipolar Possibilities (Bang or Ploop)

A lit stick of dynamite
drops to a placid lake.

Will the dynamite blow before it
reaches the surface of the water,

disturbing all serenity
in the vicinity,

or will the lake snuff out the wick
with a quick "shhh"

and swallow the dynamite whole
not much louder than a fish jumping?

Manna

Blue broccoli
could not be
more indicative

of the soil
my diet has sprung
from recently.

Red grass growing
so voracious,
everything grows stronger here.

The sunflowers drip
nectar, when apples fall
and aren't eaten,

an apple tree
always grows.
Orange sap

gushes from the maples
at times,
practically squirting.

My landscape
is a stark contrast
to others',

but pumped up
with an unparalleled
trust of nutrients,

here in the pit
of this grand valley
splitting the mountains,

I am happy
to enjoy the broken environmental
norms

effortlessly, save
climbing down
into this hole

and setting up
shack. The lily pads
in my front yard

pond grow purple,
and I no longer
fight the sucker

vines with
the same
tenacity I used to;

indeed, engorged
with rainbow
plant-blood,

I relish the opportunity
to have them available
to slice

open
and,
as with a hose,

spray the fauna
with my friends,
blasting rabbits

with front teeth
the size
of matchbooks.

From Whom All Blessings Flow

the light at the beginning and end of the tunnel,
upright posture in a crowd of hunched over backs,
the fire that burns down paper tigers,
the water that sobers up pyromaniacs,
invulnerable to attack like trying to beat up a shadow with your fists,
the answer before you ask the question,
as flexible as fluid that fills every pore,
the key from which all master keys are fashioned,
the innovation and inspiration behind every new medium of art,
the way out of the fun house,
fluent in the words of every lexicon,
strategic as a general yet gentle as a lamb.

one complete thought

the enforcer has got to die.
he is destroying all my artwork.
he burns the paintings
until the whole studio is up in flames.

the enforcer puts a sieve in front of my thoughts, and
when they come out, they are an abstract mess, not
whole and beautiful like they used to be.

He tells me how to handwrite. He tells me how to
sneeze, how to breathe, and always when it's wrong.
But also when it's right. By his definition of what right
is.

Of course, only the things that I've done without him
are the things that he approves of. The beautiful, it
seems, is always beautiful. The paradoxical nature that
defines him is made up of all of my rules and other
people's rules. But mostly my rules. Made from fears of
my inability to perform at the same level as or
supersede my past artworks. He is my rules. I know
him. I know his abstract nature, his way of clinging to
things until he destroys them.

I feel him as an angry substance in my brain. He looks
back when I don't. Grammar, he shouts! grammar! It is
difficult to tell sometimes what is him and what is a
good idea. He sticks them in my head. He is me, but I
am not him. I would like to be rid of him, his chop suey
thought processes,

his impossible to put a finger on nature

In Your Own Words

Poetry has all the implications
of fine print and is as seldom
read. It's legally binding
to the universe and poets are
the practitioners of its laws.
It's as important and unobserved
as DNA, why poets find themselves
among the most unread and quoted
people who can go unnoticed in their day,
but whose resonances echo loud enough
to turn entire languages on their heads.

Decrepit 20 Something Gurgles, "Satisfaction."

Where I live
you can find inane paparazzi
who have no one to report to
but have to get the story
and have to go back home
the same way that they came
a dime a dozen.

It's terrible for 5 o'clock traffic
and dangerous
around construction sites.

Here, people don't care
if they make sounds
that aren't words.

Round here,
some people
and hygiene
won't mix.

But in this mix
my space is nice,
I gurgle satisfactorily
as I have needed to
from so many years
of neglect, from
so many years
of a lack of care.

Down here,
my art
is acknowledged,
encouraged and
well received

to the degree
that it was supposed to be

and never
taken for granted

so I can heal
and remember
the amazing power of
wanting to make something
to delight another person or a group of people.

Faux Species

I die for your sins.
It is my super capability.
I excel at this
with moral compass tattooing CBT
throughout every one of my footsteps,
through my view out from the windows of my soul.
Like the mantis
that allows herself to be devoured alive
by its offspring in extremely polluted environments
wiped clean of nutrients,
its hormonally super-charged meat
killing their little legs instantaneously,
they spelled schizophrenia wrong,
it's spelled S-A-C-R-I-F-I-C-I-A-L-L-Y,
the degradation of all of their dead, mutated bodies
cleaning the ground about and around them,
for that we may smoke their brains,
I reenact their drama, asking,
"What can I die for you for?"
Grasshoppers dying in the sand.
They're every bit as horrible as I think they are,
these movements
of fisheries and wildlife management.

The Sound of Light

What is the sound of
darkness hushing sunlight? Of
dawn breaking darkness?

1/0

There is a moment in time directly before midnight. Time is linear; therefore, this must be true. When we think of time, we must acknowledge that in measuring time we use units which have mathematical equivalents. In pinpointing the exact moment before midnight strikes, mathematical units are of no avail, as there is no mathematical unit capable of escaping the possibility of increased specificity, which can overcome the fact that each time-related mathematical unit can be broken down into a subsequently smaller mathematical unit, not unlike cutting an object in half repeatedly. We must similarly deduce that, as language is used to express math but as math cannot express this point, language is our fundamental element of perception. For this reason, that there should exist something in math that cannot be defined mathematically, I have decided to name this moment "soul."

The Reality of the Situation

Imagine every cell phone
attached to a cord.

Pathological Learning

Do we become trapped
in our minds
if we have problems
there's no language for?

Ask us mentally ill
who naturally incur
a bit of genius
for using our brains
in ways that defy convention.

Crooked Antennae

If you go long enough
without making sense,
your brain will get
stuck that way.

Return with What You Have

Some strange kind of alchemy
returning creature comforts and to old haunts
being given the opportunity to consciously differentiate
what went wrong with my perceptions in the past
with what is real
in passing these same people, places and things
that remain unchanged. I wonder if seeing the face of God
is the same way.

Procrastinating the Profound

A lot of people
treat poets and God
by not going to either
until they feel
there is no other choice.

Expound

Like a political prisoner escaping a jail cell
living between breaths of fresh air
on his way out underground,
I live from impulse to impulse
leading to freedom of expression,
the air of something significant
undermining these charades.

Pinned Down 4-Leaf Clover in a Display Case

What determines
if someone
should be allowed
to live?

How many
and what natured transgressions
til one's plumb out of luck?
Who drops the ax?

How many years
have you felt the ax
should fall
for what you did
and/or didn't do,
what's that anticipation like?

Is it luck
we're here at all
how we are,
heredity partially mutated;
is luck a mutation
and that's why
we can never
keep it in place,
nail it down,
pin it like a butterfly
dead, preserved
and for observation
so that we may learn its effect?

sympathy for artists

much of my time
is spent recuperating
from mental
overwork
doing what
most
appreciate to some degree
once they see it,
are largely unaware of
and aren't asking me to do:
scouring the globe
for the very best parts of things,
synthesizing them
into formula so purely stimulating –
ricocheting from one pleasure center
to another, lighting up your inner switchboard
in just such a way
that in the same breath you used
to call me lazy, you'll breathe
my work, "a guilty pleasure."

On the Subject of Angels

Therapy, where everything that would keep
you from living
brings you back to life; zombies return your
brains, vampires,
your blood; demons detach themselves from
your soul;
ghosts vacate your spirit and angel armor
finally reveals itself
as forever being and having been bright in
the bones
of your friends, past loves, family, foes and
yourself.

The Beggar in My Brain

The beggar in my brain has known opulence, thousands of words are on the books, but somehow, there, where words are currency – in other words, effectual of change – the ledger keeps coming back barely in the black, usually down to my last red cent which smells of prophecy, jinx, conundrum, and bends, beggaring belief, found at the bottom of a sewer caught in hair and trash that sometimes clogs the drain. The beggar knows better than to throw it back down the toilet bowl – after having retrieved it – expecting to get anything back except clogged thoughts and comeuppance. Some wishing well. My last red cent, burning like a coal in my hand, dictates how all the others are spent that must be hidden beneath and between my metaphysical couch cushions or fallen out of holes in threadbare pockets, capital once collected in my cup.

Branching

sleepwakesleepwake
wakesleepwakesleep
sleepwakesleepwake
wakesleepwakesleep
wakesleepwakesleep
wakedreamsleepwake
sleepdreamwakesleep
wakedreamwakesleep
wakedreamsleepwake
sleepdreamsleepwake

Thank You

Mom, Laura, Myles, Thalia, Dad, Greg Bliss, Christina Slofstra, Reb Roberts, Carmel Loftis, Dave Vander Ark, Chris Schaefer, Diana Gameros, Christine Stephens-Krieger, Scott Krieger, Emily Schaefer, Quinn Davey, Nick Nortier, Shane Tripp, Lamont Arrington, Nick Kondyles, G Foster II, David Cope, Maryann Lesert, G. F. Korreck, Jack Ridl, Anthony Bell, Shaun Heeren, John Maliepaard, Linda Kaufman, Alban Fischer, Ander Monson, Deirdre Chervenka, Kelsey May, Tyler Steimle, Azizi Jasper, Robert VanderMolen, Craig Vredeveld (Root Boy), Diane Baum, Kait Polzin, Ander Monson, Carie Haizman, Kate Linares, and everyone from the following groups: extended family, Grand River Poetry Collective, the Creative Youth Center, The Litribune, the Twilight Tribe, Grand Rapids Clowns, Heartside Gallery and Studio, Schuler Books, WYCE, Literary Life, The Retort, LEAC, all of the hosts, venues, and participants of all of the open mics and poetry workshops in Grand Rapids, MI, the Noes, Roses, Wymas, DeBoers, Meyers, and Kathy O'Breen, God and all those wonderful souls thirsty for God I've met on the path to try to understand God better, and all those who have helped me along the way with poetry or just in general. Thank you.

Acknowledgments

"crux" was previously published in *Voices*

"Velvet," "mourning," "cross-pollination," "perfection to the 3rd degree, Y, and x-bound," "jay," "Laundering Purgatorial Purges," and "being" were published in *Display*

www.ingramcontent.com/pod-product-compliance
Lightning Source LLC
Chambersburg PA
CBHW051334120626
46547CB00016B/2531